HOW TO LOVE YOURS

PUTTING YOURSELF FIRST

Be One Step Ahead In
The Love Department

Rida Lester

Table of Contents

PART 1 5
Chapter 1: 6 Steps To Focus On Growth 6
Chapter 2: Understanding Yourself 11
Chapter 3: Doing The Thing You Love Most 13
Chapter 4: Things That Spark Joy 15
Chapter 5: *The Daily Routine Experts for Peak Productivity* 17
Chapter 6: How To live Your Best Life 20
Chapter 7: Happy People Are Proactive About Relationships 22
Chapter 8: Enjoying The Simple Things 25
Chapter 9: Achieving Happiness 26
Chapter 10: 8 Ways To Deal With Setbacks In Life 28
PART 2 34
Chapter 1: The Power of Contentment 35
Chapter 2: The Lure of Wanting Luxury Items 37
Chapter 3: Living in the Moment 40
Chapter 4: Hitting Rock Bottom 42
Chapter 5: How To Deal With Feelings of Unworthiness 45
Chapter 6: How To Achieve True Happiness 48
Chapter 7: The Things That Matter 52
Chapter 8: Make Friends With Your Problems 55
Chapter 9: How To Take Action 58
Chapter 10: Happy People Do What Matters to Them 61
PART 3 64
Chapter 1: Being 100% Happy Is Overrated 65
Chapter 2: The Trick To Focusing 67
Chapter 3: Having a Balanced Life 69
Chapter 4: Enjoying The Journey 71

Chapter 5: Don't Make Life Harder Than It Needs To Be 73
Chapter 6: Practicing Visualisation For Your Goals 76
Chapter 7: Happy People Live Slow 79
Chapter 8: 7 Ways To Know If You're A Good Person 81
Chapter 9: Constraints Make You Better: Why the Right Limitations Boost Performance 85
Chapter 10: Believe in Yourself 89

PART 1

Chapter 1:
6 Steps To Focus On Growth

Growth is a lifelong process. We grow every moment from the day we are born until our eventual death. And the amazing thing about growth is that there is no real limit to it.

Now, what exactly is growth? Well, growing is the process of changing from one state to another and usually, it has to be positive; constructive; better-than-before. Although growth occurs equally towards all directions in the early years of our life, the rate of growth becomes more and more narrowed down to only a few particular aspects of our life as we become old. We become more distinctified as individuals, and due to our individuality, not everyone of us can possibly grow in all directions. With our individual personality, experiences, characteristics, our areas of growth become unique to us. Consequently, our chances of becoming successful in life corresponds to how we identify our areas of growth and beam them on to our activities with precision. Let us explore some ways to identify our key areas of growth and utilize them for the better of our life.

1. **Identify Where You Can Grow**

For a human being, growth is relative. One person cannot grow in every possible way because that's how humans are—we simply cannot do every thing at once. One person may grow in one way while another may grow in a completely different way. Areas of growth can be so unlike that one's positive growth might even seem like negative growth to another person's perspective. So, it is essential that we identify the prime areas where we need to grow. This can be done through taking surveys, asking people or critically analyzing oneself. Find out what lackings do you have as a human being, find out what others think that you lack as a human being. Do different things and note down where you are weak but you have to do it anyway. Then, make a list of those areas where you need growing and move on to the next step.

2. Accept That You Need To Grow In Certain Areas

After carefully identifying your lackings, accept these in your conscious and subconscious mind. Repeatedly admit to yourself and others that you lack so and so qualities where you wish to grow with time.

Never feel ashamed of your shortcomings. Embrace them comfortably because you cannot trully change yourself without accepting that you need to change. Growth is a dynamic change that drags you way out of your comfort zone and pushes you into the wild. And to start on this endeavor for growth, you need to have courage. Growth is a choice that requires acceptance and humility.

3. Remind Yourself of Your Shortcomings

You can either write it down and stick it on your fridge or just talk about it in front of people you've just met—this way, you'll constantly keep reminding yourself that you have to grow out of your lackings. And this remembrance will tell you to try—try improving little by little. Try growing.

It is important to remain consciously aware of these at all times because you never know when you might have to face what. All the little and big things you encounter every day are all opportunities of growth. This takes us to the fourth step:

4. Face Your Problems

Whatever you encounter, in any moment or place in your life is an opportunity created: an opportunity for learning. A very old adage goes: "the more we learn, the more we grow". So, if you don't face your problems and run away from them, then you are just losing the opportunity to learn from it, and thus, losing the opportunity of growing from it. Therefore, facing whatever life throws at you also has an important implication on your overall growth. Try to make yourself useful against all odds. Even if you fail at it, you will grow anyway.

5. Cross The Boundary

So, by now you have successfully identified your areas of growth, you have accepted them, you constantly try to remind yourself of them and you face everything that comes up, head on—never running away. You are already making progress. Now comes the step where you push yourself beyond your current status. You go out of what you are already facing and make yourself appear before even more unsettling circumstances.

This is a very difficult process, but if you grow out of here, nothing can stop you ever. And only a few people successfully make it through. You create your own problems, no one might support you and yet still, you try to push forward, make yourself overcome new heights of difficulties and grow like the tallest tree in the forest. You stand out of the crowd. This can only be done in one or two subjects in a lifetime. So make sure that you know where you want to grow. Where you want to invest that much effort, and time, and dedication. Then, give everything to it. Growth is a life's journey.

6. Embrace Your Growth

After you have crossed the boundary, there is no turning back. You have achieved new heights in your life, beyond what you thought you could have ever done. The area—the subject in which you tried to develop yourself, you have made yourself uniquely specialized in that particular area. You have outgrown the others in that field. It is time for you to make yourself habituated with that and embrace it gracefully. The wisdom you've accumulated through growth is invaluable—it has its roots deeply penetrated into your life. The journey that you've gone through while pursuing your growth will now define you. It is who you are.

As I've mentioned in the first line, "growth is a lifelong process". Growth is not a walk in the park, It is you tracking through rough terrains—steep heights and unexplored depths for an entire lifetime. Follow these simple yet difficult steps; grow into the tallest tree and your life will shine upon you like the graceful summer sun.

Chapter 2:
Understanding Yourself

Today we're going to talk about a topic that hopefully helps you become more aware of who you are as a person. And why do you exist right here and right now on this Earth. Because if we don't know who we are, if we don't understand ourselves, then how can we expect to other stand and relate to others? And why we even matter?

How many of you think that you can describe yourself accurately? If someone were to ask you exactly who you are, what would you say? Most of us would say we are Teachers, doctors, lawyers, etc. We would associate our lives with our profession.

But is that really what we are really all about?

Today I want to ask you not what you do, and not let your career define you, but rather what makes you feel truly alive and connected with the world? What is it about your profession that made you want to dedicated your life and time to it? Is there something about the job that makes you want to get up everyday and show up for the work, or is it merely to collect the paycheck at the end of the month?

I believe that that there is something in each and everyone of us that makes us who we are, and keeps us truly alive and full. For those that dedicate their lives to be Teachers, maybe they see themselves as an educator, a role model, a person who is in charge of helping a kid grow up, a nurturer, a parental figure. For Doctors, maybe they see themselves as healers, as someone who feels passionate about bringing life to someone. Whatever it may be, there is more to them than their careers.

For me, I see myself as a future caregiver, and to enrich the lives of my family members. That is something that I feel is one of my purpose in life. That I was born, not to provide

Putting Yourself First

for my family monetary per se, but to provide the care and support for them in their old age. That is one of my primary objectives. Otherwise, I see and understand myself as a person who loves to share knowledge with others, as I am doing right now. I love to help others in some way of form, either to inspire them, to lift their spirits, or to just be there for them when they need a crying shoulder. I love to help others fulfill their greatest potential, and it fills my heart with joy knowing that someone has benefitted from my advice. From what I have to say. And that what i have to say actually does hold some merit, some substance, and it is helping the lives of someone out there.. to help them make better decisions, and to help the, realise that life is truly wonderful. That is who i am.

Whenever I try to do something outside of that sphere, when what I do does not help someone in some way or another, I feel a sense of dread. I feel that what I do becomes misaligned with my calling, and I drag my feet each day to get those tasks done. That is something that I have realized about myself. And it might be happening to you too.

If u do not know exactly who you are and why you are here on this Earth, i highly encourage you to take the time to go on a self-discovery journey, however long it may take, to figure that out. Only when you know exactly who you are, can you start doing the work that aligns with ur purpose and calling. I don't meant this is in a religious way, but i believe that each and every one of us are here for a reason, whether it may to serve others, to help your fellow human beings, or to share your talents with the world, we should all be doing something with our lives that is at least close to that, if not exactly that.

So I challenge each and everyone of you to take this seriously because I believe you will be much happier for it. Start aligning your work with your purpose and you will find that life is truly worth living.

Chapter 3:
Doing The Thing You Love Most

Today we are going to talk about following your heart and just going for your passion, even if it ends up being a hobby project.

Many of us have passions that we want to pursue. Whether it be a sport, a fitness goal, a career goal, or simply just doing something we know we are good at. Something that electrifies our soul. Something that really doesn't require much persuasion for us to just go do it on a whim.

Many of us dare not pursue this passion because people have told us time and time again that it will not lead to anywhere. Or maybe it is that voice inside your head that is telling you you should just stick to the practical things in life. Whatever the reasons may be, that itch always seem to pester us, calling out to us, even though we have tried our best to put it aside.

We know what our talents are, and the longer we don't put it out there in the world, the longer we keep it bottled up inside of us, the longer the we will regret it. Personally, Music has always been something that has been calling out to me since i was 15. I've always dabbled in and out of it, but never took it seriously. I found myself 14 years later, wondering how much i could've achieved in the music space if i had just leaned in to it just a little.

I decided that I had just about put it off for long enough and decided to pursue music part time. I just knew deep down inside me that if i did not at least try, that i was going to regret it at some point again in the future. It is true that passions come and go. We may jump from passion to passion over the course of our lives, and that is okay. But if that thing has been there calling out to you for years or even decades, maybe you should pay closer attention to it just a little more.

Make your passion a project. Make it a hobby. Pursue it in one form or another. We may never be able to make full careers out of our passions, but we can at least incorporate it into our daily lives like a habit. You may find ourselves happier and more fulfilled should you tap that creative space in you that has always been there.

Sure life still takes precedence. Feeding the family, earning that income, taking care of that child. But never for one second think that you should sacrifice doing what truly makes you happy for all of that other stuff, no matter how important. Even as a hobby, pursuing it maybe 30mins a day, or even just an hour a week. It is a start and it is definitely better than nothing.

At the end of the day passions are there to feed our soul. To provide it will some zest and life to our otherwise mundane lives. The next time you hear that voice again, lean in to it. Don't put it off any longer.

Chapter 4:
Things That Spark Joy

I'm sure you've heard the term "spark joy", and this is our topic of discussion today that I am going to borrow heavily from Marie Kondo.

Now why do I find the term spark joy so fascinating and why have i used it extensively in all areas of my life ever since coming across that term a few years ago?

When I first watched Marie Kondo's show on Netflix and also reading articles on how this simple concept that she has created has helped people declutter their homes by choosing the items that bring joy to them and discarding or giving away the ones that don't, I began my own process of decluttering my house of junk from clothes to props to ornaments, and even to furniture.

I realised that many things that looked good or are the most aesthetically pleasing, aren't always the most comfortable to use or wear. And when they are not my go to choice, they tend to sit on shelves collecting dust and taking up precious space in my house. And after going through my things one by one, this recurring theme kept propping up time and again. And i subconsciously associated comfort and ease of use with things that spark joy to me. If I could pick something up easily without hesitation to use or wear, they tend to me things that I gravitated to naturally, and these things began to spark joy when i used them. And when i started getting rid of things that I don't find particularly pleased to use, i felt my house was only filled with enjoyable things that I not only enjoyed looking at, but also using on a regular and frequent basis.

This association of comfort and ease of use became my life philosophy. It didn't apply to simply just decluttering my home, but also applied to the process of acquiring in the form of shopping. Every time i would pick something up and consider if it was worthy of a purpose, i would examine whether this thing would be something that I felt was comfortable and that i could see myself utilising, and if that answer was no, i would put them down and never consider them again because i knew deep down that it would not spark joy in me as I have associated joy with comfort.

This simple philosophy has helped saved me thousands of dollars in frivolous spending that was a trademark of my old self. I would buy things on the fly without much consideration and most often they would end up as white elephants in my closet or cupboard.

To me, things that spark joy can apply to work, friends, and relationships as well. Expanding on the act of decluttering put forth by Marie Kondo. If the things you do, and the people you hang out with don't spark you much joy, then why bother? You would be better off spending time doing things with people that you actually find fun and not waste everybody's time in the process. I believe you would also come out of it being a much happier person rather than forcing yourself to be around people and situations that bring you grief.

Now that is not to say that you shouldn't challenge yourself and put yourself out there. But rather it is to give you a chance to assess the things you do around you and to train yourself to do things that really spark joy in you that it becomes second nature. It is like being fine tuned to your 6th sense in a way because ultimately we all know what we truly like and dislike, however we choose to ignore these feelings and that costs us time effort and money.

So today's challenge is for you to take a look at your life, your home, your friendships, career, and your relationships. Ask yourself, does this thing spark joy? If it doesn't, maybe you should consider a decluttering of sorts from all these different areas in your life and to streamline it to a more minimalist one that you can be proud of owning each and every piece.

Take care and I'll see you in the next one.

Chapter 5:

The Daily Routine Experts for Peak Productivity

What is the one thing we want to get done for a successful life? That is an effective daily routine to go through the day, every day. History is presented as an example that every high achiever has had a good routine for their day. Some simple changes in our life can change the outcome drastically. We have to take the experts' advice for a good lifestyle. We have to choose everything, from color to college, ourselves. But an expert's advice gives us confidence in our choice.

You have to set the bar high so that you get your product at the end of the day. Experts got their peak productivity by shaping their routine in such a way that it satisfies them. The productivity expert Tim Ferriss gave us a piece of simple yet effective advice for such an outcome. He taught us the importance of controlling oneself and how essential it is to provide yourself with a non-reactive practice. When you know how to control yourself, life gets more manageable, as it gives you the power to prevent many things. It reduces stress which gets your productivity out.

Another productive expert of ours, Cal Newport, gives us his share of information. He is always advising people to push themselves to their limits. He got successful by giving his deep work more priority than other work. He is managing multitasks at the same time while being a husband and a father. He is a true example of a good routine that leads to positive productivity. It would help if you decided what matters to you the most and need to focus on that. Get your priorities straight and work toward those goals. Construct your goals and have a clear idea of what your next step will be. It will result in increasing your confidence.

Now, the questions linger that how to start your day? Early is the answer. Early to bed and early to rising has been the motto of productive people. As Dan Ariely said, there is a must 3 hours in our day when our productivity is at its peak. A morning person hit more products, as it's said that sunrise is when you get active. Mostly from 8 o'clock to 10 o'clock. It's said that morning is the time when our minds work the sharpest. It provides you alertness and good memory ability. It is also called the "protected time." We get a new sense to think from, and then we get a sound vision of our steps and ideas to a routine of peak productivity.

Charles Duhigg is a known news reporter, works for the New York Times. He tells us to stop procrastinating and visualizing our next step in life. Not only does it give you confidence, but it also gives you a satisfactory feeling. You get an idea of the result, and you tend to do things more that way. This way, you get habitual of thinking about your next step beforehand. Habits are gradually formed. They are difficult to change but easy to assemble. A single practice can bring various elements from it. Those elements can help you learn the routine of an expert.

You will eventually fall into place. No one can change themselves in one day. Hard work is the key to any outcome. Productivity is the result of many factors but, an excellent daily routine is an integral part of it which we all need to follow. Once you fall into working constantly, you won't notice how productive you have become. It becomes a habit. There might be tough decisions along the way, which is typical for an average life. We need to focus on what's in front of us and start with giving attention to one single task on top of your priority list. That way, you can achieve more in less time. These are some factors and advice to start a daily routine for reaching the peak of productivity with the help of some great products.

Chapter 6:
How To live Your Best Life

This is a simple yet not easy topic to tackle. But I am sure that this question is something that all of you are aspiring to achieve in life. Because really, being on earth, being alive, it does not have any real significance if we do not live it to our fullest potential, to enjoy every single wonderful thing that life has to offer, to smell the flowers, to see the sights along the way, and to appreciate the little things while going for the big dreams.

For many of us, I do believe that it was a lot easier to live our best life while we were in school. Whilst the pressure of school and getting good grades were always constantly hanging over us, that was the case for every other kid around us. It was fair game. And we all strived to be the best student that we could possibly be. At the same time we had time to pursue our interests, learn new things, learn new skills, and even new instruments. The possibilities were endless and the world was our oyster. We explored the deepest oceans and in my opinion, we were indeed living our best lives as children and teens.

Making friends and hanging out with them frequently either through study or play weren't difficult. We were social creatures and we were really good at that.

However as we grew older, into our twenties and beyond, we start to lose that spark. That wonder. That curiosity. That vision that the world was in the palm of our hands. Instead, that view became more myopic, it keeps shrinking, work gets in the way, and we lose our sense of wonder and curiosity. We become more cynical and dull. And we stopped really trying to live our best life.

The introvert in us starts to come out more and more, and we retreat into our homes watching Netflix and YouTube, rather than going out there into the world and doing

Putting Yourself First

something significant or fun. In today's topic we are not going to talk about careers or income, because i do not believe that you need to be incredibly successful monetarily to be described as living your best life. But rather it's the other things that make up who you are that matters here.

And for many of us, it has become all too easy to retreat into the comfort of our home after a long day's work and decide that it is perfectly good to just lay on our couches and do nothing all day or weekend. We gradually disconnect ourselves from the outside world and we live in our own little bubble. And we think it is okay.

However what we fail to realize is that over time, these hours add up to days, weeks, months, and even years. And we realise that at the end of it all, we have nothing to show for it. We have not put ourselves in positions where we are exposed to new experiences and things. Of fostering meaningful friendships that would last u to till the end of your life. And we find ourselves alone and regretting that we had not utilised our time more wisely to build up those relationships or creating those experiences that we can look back on and say I'm glad i did all those things. I'm glad i left no stone unturned. I'm glad i did not waste my time doing nothing.

So to sum it all up, i believe that to live your best life, we should all look back at our middle school and high school days. What were we doing then that made everything so interesting and exciting, and how can we integrate more of that into our lives instead of choosing isolation. Whether that be trying out a new activity, learning a new sport, or even simply just hanging out with friends that you can rely on on a much more regular basis. I do believe that you will start to feel that life has much more meaning and happiness will soon follow.

I'll leave it at that today. I hope you guys learned something new today and I'll see you in the next one. Take care!

Chapter 7:
Happy People Are Proactive About Relationships

Researchers have found that as human beings we are only capable of maintaining up to 150 meaningful relationships, including five primary, close relationships.

This holds true even with the illusion of thousands of "friends" on social media platforms such as Facebook, Instagram, and Twitter. If you think carefully about your real interactions with people, you'll find the five close/150 extended relationships rule holds true.

Perhaps not coincidentally, Tony Robbins, the personal development expert, and others argue that your attitudes, behavior, and success in life are the sum total of your five closest relationships. So, toxic relationships, toxic life.

With this in mind, it's essential to continue to develop relationships that are positive and beneficial. **But in today's distracted world, these relationships won't just happen.**

We need to be proactive about developing our relationships.

Putting Yourself First

My current favorite book on personal development is Tim Ferriss's excellent, though long, 700+ page book, *Tools of Titans: The Tactics, Routines, and Habits of Billionaires, Icons, and World-Class Performers.*

At one point, Ferriss quotes retired women's volleyball great Gabby Reece:

I always say that I'll go first.... That means if I'm checking out at the store, I'll say "hello" first. If I'm coming across somebody and make eye contact, I'll smile first. [I wish] people would experiment with that in their life a little bit: be first, because – not all times, but most times – it comes in your favor... The response is pretty amazing.... I was at the park the other day with the kids.

Oh, my God. Hurricane Harbor [water park]. It's like hell. There were these two women a little bit older than me. We couldn't be more different, right? And I walked by them, and I just looked at them and smiled. The smile came to their face so instantly. They're ready, but you have to go first because now we're being trained in this world [to opt out] – nobody's going first anymore.

Be proactive: start the conversation

I agree. I was excited to read this principle because I adopted this by default years ago, and it's given me the opportunity to hear the most amazing stories and develop the greatest relationships you can imagine.

On airplanes, in the grocery store, at lunch, I've started conversations that led to trading heartfelt stories, becoming friends, or doing business together. A relationship has to start someplace, and that can be any place in any moment.

Be proactive: lose your fear of being rejected
I also love this idea because it will help overcome one of the main issues I hear from my training and coaching clients – the fear of making an initial connection with someone they don't know.

This fear runs deep for many people and may be hardwired in humans. We are always observing strangers to determine if we can trust them – whether they have positive or dangerous intent.

In addition, **we fear rejection. Our usual negative self-talk says something like,** *If I start the conversation, if I make eye contact, if I smile, what if it's not returned?*

What if I'm rejected, embarrassed, or ignored by no response? I'll feel like an idiot, a needy loser.

Chapter 8:
Enjoying The Simple Things

Today we're going to talk about a topic that might sound cheesy, but trust me it's worth taking a closer look at. And that is how we should strive to enjoy the simple things in life.

Many of us think we need a jam packed schedule for the week, month, or year, to tell us that we are leading a very productive and purposeful life. We find ways to fill our time with a hundred different activities. Going to this event, that event, never slowing down. And we find ourselves maybe slightly burnt out by the end of it.

We forget that sometimes simplicity is better than complication. Have you sat down with your family for a simple lunch meal lately? You don't have to talk, you just have to be in each other's company and enjoying the food that is being served in front of you.

I found myself appreciating these moments more than I did running around to activities thinking that I needed something big to be worth my time. I found sitting next to my family on the couch watching my own shows while they watch theirs very rewarding. I found eating alone at my favourite restaurant while watching my favourite sitcom to be equally as enjoyable as hanging out with a group of 10 friends. I also found myself richly enjoying a long warm shower every morning and evening. It is the highlights of my day.

My point is that we need to start looking at the small things we can do each day that will bring us joy. Things that are within our control. Things that we know can hardly go wrong. This will provide some stability to gain some pleasure from. The little nuggets in the day that will not be determined by external factors such as the weather, friends bailing on us, or irritating customers.

When we focus on the little things, we make life that much better to live through.

Chapter 9:
Achieving Happiness

Happiness is a topic that is at the core of this channel. Because as humans we all want to be happy in some way shape or form. Happiness strikes as something that we all want to strive for because how can we imagine living an unhappy life. It might be possible but it wouldn't be all that fun no matter how you spin it. However I'm gonna offer another perspective that would challenge the notion of happiness and one that maybe would be more attainable for the vast majority of people.

So why do we as humans search for happiness? It is partly due to the fact that it has been ingrained in us since young that we all should strive to live a happy and healthy life. Happiness has become synonymous with the very nature of existence that when we find ourselves unhappy in any given moment, we tend to want to pivot our life and the current situation we are in to one that is more favourable, one that is supposedly able to bring us more happiness.

But how many of us are actually always happy all the time? I would argue that happiness is not at all sustainable if we were feeling it at full blast constantly. After a while we would find ourselves being numb to it and maybe that happiness would turn into neutrality or even boredom. There were times in my life where i felt truly happy and free. I felt that i had great friends around me, life had limitless possibilities, the weather was great, the housing situation was great, and i never wanted it to end as i knew that it was the best time of my life.

However knowing that this circumstance is only temporary allowed me to cherish each and every moment more meaningfully. As i was aware that time was not infinite and that some day this very state of happiness would somehow end one way or another, that i would use that time wisely and spend them with purpose and meaning. And it was

Putting Yourself First

this sense that nothing ever lasts forever that helped me gain a new perspective on everything i was doing at that present moment in time. Of course, those happy times were also filled with times of trials, conflicts, and challenges, and they made that period of my life all the more memorable and noteworthy.

For me, happiness is a temporary state that does not last forever. We might be happy today but sad tomorrow, but that is perfectly okay and totally fine. Being happy all the time is not realistic no matter how you spin it. The excitement of getting a new house and new car would soon fade from the moment you start driving in it, and that happiness you once thought you associated with it can disappear very quickly. And that is okay. Because life is about constant change and nothing really ever stays the same.

With happiness comes with it a whole host of different emotions that aims to highlight and enhance its feeling. Without sadness and sorrow, happiness would have no counter to be matched against. It is like a yin without a yang. And we need both in order to survive.

I believe that to be truly happy, one has to accept that sadness and feelings of unhappiness will come as a package deal. That whilst we want to be happy, we must also want to feel periods of lull to make the experience more rewarding.

I challenge all of you today to view happiness as not something that is static and that once you achieved it that all will be well and life will be good, but rather a temporary state of feeling that will come again and again when you take steps to seek it.

I also want to bring forth to you an alternative notion to happiness, in the form of contentment, that we will discuss in the next video. Take care and I'll see you there.

Chapter 10:
8 Ways To Deal With Setbacks In Life

Life is never the same for anyone - It is an ever-changing phenomenon, making you go through all sorts of highs and lows. And as good times are an intrinsic part of your life, so are bad times. One day you might find yourself indebted by 3-digit figures while having only $40 in your savings account. Next day, you might be vacationing in Hawaii because you got a job that you like and pays $100,000 a year. There's absolutely no certainty to life (except passing away) and that's the beauty of it. You never know what is in store for you. But you have to keep living to see it for yourself. Setbacks in life cannot be avoided by anyone. Life will give you hardships, troubles, break ups, diabetes, unpaid bills, stuck toilet and so much more. It's all a part of your life.

Here's 8 ways that you might want to take notes of, for whenever you may find yourself in a difficult position in dealing with setback in life.

1. **Accept and if possible, embrace it**

The difference between accepting and embracing is that when you accept something, you only believe it to be, whether you agree or disagree. But when you embrace something, you truly KNOW it to be true and accept it as a whole. There is no dilemma or disagreement after you have embraced something.

So, when you find yourself in a difficult situation in life, accept it for what it is and make yourself whole-heartedly believe that this problem in your life, at this specific time, is a part of your life. This problem is what makes you complete. This problem is meant for you and only you can go through it. And you will. Period. There can be no other way.

The sooner you embrace your problem, the sooner you can fix it. Trying to bypass it will only add upon your headaches.

2. **Learn from it**

Seriously, I can't emphasize how important it is to LEARN from the setbacks you face in your life. Every hardship is a learning opportunity. The more you face challenges, the more you grow. Your capabilities expand with every issue you solve—every difficulty you go through, you rediscover yourself. And when you finally deal off with it, you are reborn. You are a new person with more wisdom and experience.

When you fail at something, try to explore why you failed. Be open-minded about scrutinizing yourself. Why couldn't you overcome a certain situation? Why do you think of this scenario as a 'setback'? The moment you find the answers to these questions is the moment you will have found the solution.

3. Execute What You Have Learnt

The only next step from here is to execute that solution and make sure that the next time you face a similar situation, you'll deal with it by having both your arms tied back and blindfolded. All you have to do is remember what you did in a similar past experience and reapply your previous solution.

Thomas A. Edison, the inventor of the light bulb, failed 10,000 times before finally making it. And he said "I have not failed. I just found 10,000 ways that won't work".

The lesson here is that you have to take every setback as a lesson, that's it.

4. Without shadow, you can never appreciate light

This metaphor is applicable to all things opposite in this universe. Everything has a reciprocal; without one, the other cannot exist. Just as without shadow, we wouldn't have known what light is, similarly, without light, we could've never known about shadow. The two opposites identify and complete each other.

Too much of philosophy class, but to sum it up, your problems in life, ironically, is exactly why you can enjoy your life. For example, if you are a chess player, then defeating other chess players will give you enjoyment while getting defeated will give you distress. But, when you are a chess prodigy—you have defeated every single chess player on earth and there's no one else to defeat, then what will you do to derive pleasure? Truth is, you can now no longer enjoy chess. You have no one to defeat. No one gives you the fear of losing anymore and as a result, the taste of winning has lost its appeal to you.

So, whenever you face a problem in life, appreciate it because without it, you can't enjoy the state of not having a problem. Problems give you the pleasure of learning from them and solving them.

5. View Every Obstacle As an opportunity

This one's especially for long term hindrances to your regular life. The COVID-19 pandemic for instance, has set us back for almost two years now. As distressing it is, there is also some positive impact of it. A long-term setback opens up a plethora of new avenues for you to explore. You suddenly get a large amount of time to experiment with things that you have never tried before.

When you have to pause a regular part of your life, you can do other things in the meantime. I believe that every one of us has a specific talent and most people never know what their talent is simply because they have never tried that thing.

6. Don't Be Afraid to experiment

People pursue their whole life for a job that they don't like and most of them never ever get good at it. As a result, their true talent gets buried under their own efforts. Life just carries on with unfound potential. But when some obstacle comes up and frees you from the clutches of doing what you have been doing for a long time, then you should get around and experiment. Who knows? You, a bored high school teacher, might be a natural at tennis. You won't know it unless you are fired from that job and actually play tennis to get over it. So whenever life gives you lemons, quit trying to hold on to it. Move on and try new things instead.

7. Stop Comparing yourself to others

The thing is, we humans are emotional beings. We become emotionally vulnerable when we are going through something that isn't supposed to be. And in such times, when we see other people doing fantastic things in life, it naturally makes us succumb to more self-loathing. We think lowly of our own selves and it is perfectly normal to feel this way. Talking and comapring ourselves to people who are seemingly untouched by setbacks is a counterproductive move. You will listen to their success-stories and get depressed—lose self-esteem. Even if they try their best to advise you, it won't get through to you. You won't be able to relate to them.

8. Talk to people other people who are having their own setbacks in life

I'm not asking you to talk to just any people. I'm being very specific here: talk to people who are going through bad times as well.

If you start talking to others who are struggling in life, perhaps more so compared to you, then you'll see that everyone else is also having difficulties in life. It will seem natural to you. Moreover, having talked with others might even show you that you are actually doing better than all these other people. You can always find someone who is dealing with more trouble than you and that will enlighten you. That will encourage you. If someone else can deal with tougher setbacks in life, why can't you?

Besides, listening to other people will give you a completely new perspective that you can use for yourself if you ever find yourself in a similar situation as others whom you have talked with.

Conclusion

Setbacks are a part of life. Without them we wouldn't know what the good times are. Without them we wouldn't appreciate the success that we have gotten. Without them we wouldn't cherish the moments that got us to where we are heading to. And without them there wouldn't be any challenge to fill our souls with passion and fire. Take setbacks as a natural process in the journey. Use it to fuel your drive. Use it to move your life forward one step at a time.

PART 2

Chapter 1:
The Power of Contentment

Today we're going to talk about why contentment is possibly a much more attainable and sustainable alternative than trying to achieve happiness.

As we have briefly gone through in the previous video, happiness is a state of mind that is fleeting and never truly lasts for too very long before the opposing forces of sadness and feelings of boredom start creeping in.

Happiness is a limited resource that needs energy and time to build, and we can never really be truly happy all the time. But what about the notion of contentment?

Contentment is a state of feeling that you are satisfied with the current situation and it need not go beyond that. When we say we are contented with our circumstances, with our jobs, with our friends, family, and relationships, we are telling ourselves that we have enough, and that we can and should be grateful for the things we have instead of feeling lacking in the things we don't.

Many a times when i ask myself if i am happy about something, be it a situation that I had found myself in, or the life that I am living, majority of the time the answer is a resounding no. And it is not because I am unhappy per se, but if i were to ask myself honestly, I can't bring myself to say that yes absolutely that all is great and that I am 100$% truly happy with everything. I have to say that this is my own personal experience and it may not be an accurate representation of how you see life.

However, if i were to reframe and ask myself this question of "Am I Contented with my life?" I can with absolute confidence say yes I am. I may not have everything in the world, but i can most definitely say I am contented with my job, my friends, my family, my career, my relationships, and my health and body. That I do not need to keep chasing perfection in order to be contented with myself.

You will find that as you ask yourself more and more if you are contented, and if the answer is mostly a yes, you will gradually feel a shift towards a feeling that actually life is pretty good. And that your situation is actually very favourable. Yes you may not be happy all the time, but then again who is? As long as you are contented 90% of the time, you have already won the game of life. And when you pair contentment with a feeling of gratefulness of the things you have, you will inevitably feel a sense of happiness without having to ask yourself that question or be trying to chase it down on a daily basis.

Many a times when I looked at my current situation to see if I was on the right track, I look around me and I feel that whilst there may be areas that I am lacking and certainly needs improvement, in the grand scheme of things, I am pretty well off and i am contented.

So I challenge all of you today to look at your life in a different perspective. Start asking yourself the right question of "are you contented", and if by any chance you are not majority of the time, look at what you can do to change things up so that you do feel that life is indeed great and worth living.

I wish you guys all the success in life and I'll see you in the next one. Take care.

Chapter 2:
The Lure of Wanting Luxury Items

Have you ever walked by a store and pondered over those LV bags if you were a lady? Secretly hoping that you can get your hands on one of those bags so that you can feel good about yourself when you carry them on your shoulders? Or have you ever glanced at a boutique watch shop if you were a guy hoping that you can get your hands on one of the rolexes which costs north of $10k minimum? That could be the same lust and desire for the latest and greatest cars, apple products, clothing, etc. anything you name it.

You think of saving up a year's worth of salary just to be able to afford one of these things and you see yourself feeling good about it and that you can brag to your friends and show off to people that you have the latest and most expensive product on the market. and you imagine yourself being happy that it is all you will need to stay happy.

I am here to tell you that the lure of owning luxury items can only make you happy to a certain extent. And only if purchasing these things is something of great meaning to you, like achieving a big milestone that you want to commemorate in life. In that instance, walking into that store to purchase that luxury product can be a great experience and of great significance as well. Whether it be a birthday gift to yourself, or commemorating a wedding anniversary, job/career work milestone, or any of that in nature, you will tend to hold these products with great sentimental value and hardly will you ever sell these items should the opportunity arise to make a profit from them (which is generally not the case with most things you buy).

I will argue that when you pick these products to wear from your wardrobe, you will indeed be filled with feelings of happiness, but it is not the product itself that makes you happy, but it is the story behind it, the hard work, the commemorative occasion that you will associate and remember these products for. It will transport you back in time to that place in your life when you made the purchase and you will indeed relive that emotion that took you there to the store in the first place. That to me is a meaningful luxury purchase that is not based on lust or greed, but of great significance.

But what if you are just someone who is chasing these luxury products just because everyone else has it? When you walk down the street and you see all these people carrying these products and you just tell yourself you have to have it or else? You find all the money you can dig from your savings and emergency fund to pay for that product? I would argue that in that instance, you will not be as happy as you thought you would be. These kinds of wants just simply do not carry the weight of any importance. And after feeling good for a few days after you owned that luxury good, you feel a deep sense of emptiness because it really does not make you a happier person. Instead you are someone trying to have something but with that comes a big hole in your wallet or your bank account. The enthusiasm and excitement starts to fade away and you wonder whats the next luxury good you need to buy to feel that joy again.

You see, material goods cannot fill us with love and happiness. Luxury goods are only there to serve one purpose, to reward you for your hard work and that you can comfortably purchase it without regret and worry that you are left financially in trouble. The lure of many of us is that we tend to want what we can't have. It could also turn into an obsession for many of us where we just keep buying more and more of these luxury goods to satisfy our craving for materialistic things. You will realise one day that the pursuit never ends, the more you see, the more you want. And that is just how our brains are wired.

I have a confession to make, I had an obsession for apple products myself and I always thought I wanted the latest and greatest apple products every year when a new model comes out. And every year apple seems to know how to satisfy my lust for these products and manages to make me spend thousands of dollars every time they launch something new. This addiction i would say lasted for a good 8 years until I recently realised that the excitement ALWAYS fades after a week or two. Sure it is exciting to

Putting Yourself First

play with it for a couple of days while your brain gets used to this incredible piece of technology sitting in front of you. But after a week or two, I am left wondering, whats next? I began to realise that what really made me happy was doing what i love, engaging in my favourite hobbies, meeting friends, and just living simply without so many wants in life. When you have less wants, you automatically go into a mindset of abundance. And that is a great feeling to have.

I challenge all of you today to question what is your real motivation behind wanted to buy luxury items. Is it to commemorate a significant achievement in your life? or is it a meaningless lust for something that you want to emulate others for. Dig deeper and you will find the answer. Thank you

Chapter 3:
Living in the Moment

Today we're going to talk about a topic that will help those of you struggling with fears and anxieties about your past and even about your future. And I hope that at the end of this video, you may be able to live a life that is truly more present and full.

So what is living in the moment all about and why should we even bother?

You see, for many of us, since we're young, we've been told to plan for our future. And we always feel like we're never enough until we achieve the next best grade in class, get into a great university, get a high paying career, and then retire comfortably. We always look at our life as an endless competition, and that we believe that there will always be more time to have fun and enjoy life later when we have worked our asses off and clawed our way to success. Measures that are either set by our parents, society, or our peers. And this constant desire to look ahead, while is a good motivator if done in moderation and not obsessively, can lead us to always being unhappy in our current present moment.

Because we are always chasing something bigger, the goal post keeps moving farther and farther away every time we reach one. And the reality is that we will never ever be happy with ourselves at any point if that becomes our motto. We try to look so far ahead all the time that we miss the beautiful sights along the way. We miss the whole point of our goals which is not to want the end goal so eagerly, but to actually enjoy the process, enjoy the journey, and enjoy each step along the way. The struggles, the sadness, the accomplishments, the joy. When we stop checking out the flowers around us, and when we stop looking around the beautiful sights, the destination becomes less amazing.

Putting Yourself First

Reminding ourselves to live in the present helps us keep things in perspective that yes, even though our ultimate dream is to be this and that career wise, or whatever it may be, that we must not forget that life is precious and that each day is a blessing and that we should cherish each living day as if it were your last.

Forget the idea that you might have 30 years to work before you can tell ur self that you can finally relax and retire. Because you never know if you will even have tomorrow. If you are always reminded that life is fragile and that your life isn't always guaranteed, that you become more aware that you need to live in the moment in order to live your best life. Rid yourself of any worries, anxieties, and fears you have about the future because the time will come when it comes. Things will happen for you eventually so long as you do what you need to do each and every day without obsessing over it.

Sometimes our past failures and shortcomings in the workplace can have an adverse effect on how we view the present as well. And this cycle perpetuates itself over and over again and we lose sight of what's really important to us. Our family, our friends, our pets, and we neglect them or neglect to spend enough time with them thinking we have so much time left. But we fail to remember again that life does not always work the way we want it to. And we need to be careful not to fall into that trap that we have complete and total control over our life and how our plans would work out.

In the next video we will talk about how to live in the moment if you have anxieties and fears about things unrelated to work. Whether it be a family issue or a health issue. I want to address that in a separate topic.

I hope you learned something in this short video and I'll see you in the next one. Thank you

Chapter 4:
Hitting Rock Bottom

Today we're going to talk about a topic that I hope none of you will have to experience at any point in your lives. It can be a devastating and painful experience and I don't wish it on my worst enemy, but if this happens to be you, I hope that in today's video I can help you get out of the depths and into the light again.

First of all, I'm not going to waste any more time but just tell you that hitting rock bottom could be your blessing in disguise. You see when we hit rock bottom, the only reason that we know we are there is because we have become aware and have admitted to ourselves that there is no way lower that we can go. That we know deep in our hearts that things just cannot get any worse than this. And that revelation can be enlightening. Enlightening in the sense that by simple law of physics, the worse that can happen moving forward is either you move sideways, or up. When you have nothing more left to lose, you can be free to try and do everything in your power to get back up again.

For a lot of us who have led pretty comfortable lives, sometimes it feels like we are living in a bubble. We end up drifting through life on the comforts of our merits that we fail to stop learning and growing as people. We become so jaded about everything that life becomes bland. We stop trying to be better, we stop trying to care, and we that in itself could be poison. It is like a frog getting boiled gradually, we don't notice it until it is too late and we are cooked. We are in fact slowly dying and fading into irrelevance.

But when you are at rock bottom, you become painfully aware of everything. Painfully aware of maybe your failed relationships, the things you did and maybe the people you hurt that have led you to this point. You become aware that you need to change yourself first, that everything starts with growing and learning again from scratch, like a baby learning how to walk again. And that could be a very rewarding time in your life when you become virtually fearless to try and do anything in your power to get back on your feet again.

Of course all this has to come from you. That you have to make the decision that things will never stay the same again. That you will learn from your mistakes and do the right things. When you've hit rock bottom, you can slowly begin the climb one step at a time.

Start by defining the first and most important thing that you cannot live without in life. If family means the most to you, reach out to them. Find comfort and shelter in them and see if they are able to provide you with any sort of assistance while you work on your life again. I always believe that if family is the most important thing, and that people you call family will be there with you till the very end. If family is not available to you, make it a priority to start growing a family. Family doesn't mean you have to have blood relations. Family is whoever you can rely on in your darkest times. Family is people who will accept you and love you for who you are inspite of your shortcomings. Family is people that will help nurture and get you back on your own two feet again. If you don't have family, go get one.

If hitting rock bottom to you means that you feel lost in life, in your career and finance, that you maybe lost your businesses and are dealing with the aftermath, maybe your first priority is to simply find a simple part time job that can occupy your time and keep you sustained while you figure out what to do next. Sometimes all we need is a little break to clear our heads and to start afresh again. Nothing ever stays the same. Things will get better. But don't fall into the trap of ruminating on your losses as it can be very destructive on your mental health. The past has already happened and you cannot take it back. Take stock of the reasons and don't make the same mistakes again in your career and you will be absolutely fine.

If you feel like you've hit rock bottom because of a failed marriage or relationship, whether it be something you did or your partner did, I know this can be incredibly painful and it feels like you've spent all your time with someone with nothing to show for it but wasted time and energy, but know that things like that happen and that it is perfectly normal. Humans are flawed and we all make mistakes. So yes it is okay to morn over the loss of the relationship and feel like you can't sink any lower, but don't lose faith as you will find someone again.

If hitting rock bottom is the result of you being ostracised by people around you for not being a good person, where you maybe have lost all the relationships in your life because of something you did, I'm sure you know the first step to do is to accept that you need to change. Don't look to someone else to blame but look inwards instead. Find time where you can go away on your way to reflect on what went wrong. Start going through the things that people were unhappy with you about and start looking for ways to improve yourself. If you need help, I am here for you. If not, maybe you might want to seek some professional help as well to dig a little deeper and to help guide you along a better path.

Hitting rock bottom is not a fun thing, and I don't want to claim that I know every nuance and feeling of what it means to get there, but I did feel like that once when my business failed on me and I made the decision that I could only go up from here. I started to pour all my time and energy into proving to myself that I will succeed no matter what and that I will not sit idly by and feel sorry for myself. It was a quite a journey but I came out of it stronger than before and realized that I was more resourceful than I originally thought.

So I challenge each and everyone of you who feels like you've hit the bottom to not be afraid of taking action once again. To be fearless and just take that next right step forward no matter what. And I hope to see you on the top of the mountain in time to come.

I hope you've learned something today. Take care and I'll see you in the next one.

Chapter 5:
How To Deal With Feelings of Unworthiness

Today we're going to talk about a topic that I hope none of you struggle with. But if you do, I hope to bring some light into your life today. Because i too have had to deal with such feelings before, as recently as a year ago actually.

So before we get into the solutions, we must first understand where these feelings of unworthiness comes form. And we must be aware of them before we can make changes in our lives that brings us out of that state of mind.

Let's start with my life, maybe you will understand the kinds of struggles that I had gone through that led me to feeling unworthy.

Just about 3 years ago, I started my entrepreneurial journey, a journey that was full of excitement and curiousity. After being through a couple of internships at a company, i knew the corporate life wasn't really my thing, and i set out on my own path to making money online... To see if i could find a way to have an income without having to work a 9-5 job. The start was rough as I had no experience whatsoever. But over time i started to find a bit of footing and I made some decent income here and there that would sustain my livelihood for a while. As I was starting to see some success, my "world" came crashing down as something happened with the small business that I had spent almost 3 years building up. And suddenly my income was gone. And I realized I had nothing to show for my 3 years of work. It left me feeling incredibly depressed... Although it doesnt sound like the end of the world to many of you, i felt like i had been set back many years behind my peers who were by then already steadily climbing up the corporate ladder. Feelings that I had made a grave mistake in terms of career choice started creeping up on me. As I tried to figure out what to do with my life, I couldn't help but compare my income to the income that my friends were making. And I felt did feel worthless, and inferior. And I started questioning my whole journey and life choices up till that point.

I started wondering if I was ever going to climb my way back up again, if I would ever figure out how these things actually worked, and all those negative thoughts came day in and out. Eating me alive inside.

It was only after I had done some introspection did I finally started to learn to love myself. And to learn that my journey is unique and mine alone. That I didn't need to, and must not, compare myself to others, did i really start to feel worthy again. I started to believe in my own path, and I felt proud that I had dared to try something that most of my peers were afraid to even try. I found new qualities in myself that I didn't knew I had and I started to forge a new path for myself in my own entrepreneurial journey. Eventually my experience making money online helped me claw my way back up the income ladder, and I have never looked backed since.

For me personally, the one thing that I could take away from my own experience with unworthiness, is to not compare yourself with others. You will never be happy comparing with your peers on income, relationship status, number of friends, number of followers on social media, and all that random things. If you always look at your friends in that way, you will always feel inferior because there will always be someone better than you. Sure you can look to them for inspiration and tips, but never feel that they are superior to you in anyway.. because you are unique in your own beautiful way. You should focus on your own journey and how you can be a better version of yourself. Your peers might have different sets of skills, talents, and expertise, that helped them excel in their fields, but you have your own talents too that you should exploit. You never know what you can achieve until you truly believe in yourself and fully utilise your potential.

Putting Yourself First

For you, your struggle with unworthiness could stem from the way your parents compare you to your siblings, or feeling hopeless trying to find love in this cruel world, or being rejected by companies in your Job applications, or rejection by a potential suitor. These are all valid things that can bring us down. But never let these people tell you what you can or cannot do. Prove to them that you are worthy by constantly improving yourself, mentally, physically, health wise, being emotionally resilient, grow your wisdom, and always love yourself. People cannot love you if you do not love yourself first. That is a quote that i believe very deeply.

No amount of validation from external sources can match the love that I decide to give to myself first.

If you find yourself in situations where you are being bombarded with negativity, whether it be from friends or family, i suggest you take a step back from these people. Find a community where your achievements are celebrated and appreciated, and where you can also offer the same amount of encouragement to others. Join meetup groups in your area with people of similar interests and just enjoy the journey. You will get there eventually if you believe in yourself.

So I challenge each and every one of you to always choose yourself first, look at your own journey as a unique path, different from everybody else, follow your dreams, take action, and never give up. That is the only way to prove to yourself and to the world that you are the most worthy person on the planet.

I hope you learned something today, take care and I'll see you in the next one.

Chapter 6:
How To Achieve True Happiness

How many of us actually know what happiness really is? And how many of us spend our whole lives searching for it but never seem to be happy?

I want to share with you my story today of how i stumbled upon true happiness and how you can achieve the same for yourself in your life.

Many of us go through the motion of trying to earn money because we think the more money we have, the better our lives will be. We chase the dream of increasing our earning power so that we can afford to buy nicer and more expensive things. And we believe that when we have more money, our happiness level will increase as well and we will be filled with so much money and happiness that we can finally stop chasing it.

Now I just wanna say, Yes, for those who come from a not so affluent background where they have a family to feed and basic needs have to be met to in order for them to survive, having a monetary goal to work towards is truly commendable as their drive, motivation, and sole purpose comes from supporting their family. Their sense of achievement, joy, and happiness comes from seeing their loved ones attaining basic needs and then go on to achieve success later in life at the expense of their time and energy. But they are more than okay with that and they do so with a willing heart, mind, and soul. You might even say that these people have achieved true happiness. Not because they are chasing more money, but because they are using that money to serve a greater purpose other than themselves.

But what about the rest of us who seemingly have everything we could ever want but never seem to be happy? We work hard at our jobs every single day waiting for our next promotion so that we can command a higher pay. And as our income grows, so does our appetite and desire for more expensive material things.

For guys we might chase that fancy new watch like rolex, omega, breitling, drooling over that model that always seem to be on a never-ending waitlist. And as we purchased one, feeling that temporary joy and satisfaction, we quickly look towards that next model as the shiny object we have starts to slowly fade. We lose our so-called happiness in time and We go back to work dreaming about that next watch just to feel that joy and excitement again. This could apply to other material things such as a shiny new technology gadgets smartphones, tv, and even cars.

For women, while might not be true for everyone, They might look towards that designer shoe, that branded handbag, ar that fancy jewellery that costs thousands of dollars to purchase but happily pay for it because they think it makes them feel better about ourselves. Or they could even use these purchases as retail therapy from their stressful lives and jobs.

Whatever these expensive purchases may be, we think that by spend our hard earned money on material things, it will bring us happiness and joy, but somehow it never does, and in most cases it is only temporary satisfactions.

That was exactly what happened with me. I kept chasing a higher income thinking it would bring me happiness. As a lover of technology, I always sought to buy the latest gadgets I could get my hands on. The excitement peaks and then fades. For me I realised that I had created an endless loop of trying to chase happiness but always coming up short.

One day I sat down and reflected on what exactly made me REALLY happy and I started writing down a list.

Putting Yourself First

My List Came down to these in no particular order: Spending time with family, spending time with friends, helping others, having a purpose in life, being at peace with myself, working on my own dreams, singing and making music, exercising, being grateful, and finally being a loving person to others.

As I went through this list, I realised that hey, in none of the list did i write "making more money" or "buying more things". And it finally dawned on me that these are REALLY the things that made me truly happy. And only after I had defined these things did i actively choose to do more of them every single day.

I started spending more quality time with my friends and family, i started playing my favourite sport (Tennis) a few times a week, I chose to be grateful that I can even be alive on this earth, and I chose to be more loving and humble. Finally I also actively chose not to compare myself to people who were more "successful" than I was because comparing yourself to others can NEVER make you happy and will only make you feel inferior when you are not. Always remember that You are special, you are unique, and you are amazing.

After doing these things every single day, I had become a much happier person. It is all about perspective.

So what can you do to achieve happiness for yourself?

I recommend that you do the same thing I did which is to write down a list under the title "When Am I The Happiest?" or "When Was A Time When I Truly Felt Happy?" Start breaking down these memories as you recall your past, and down the essence of the memory. Everybody's list will be different as happiness means different things to every one of us. Once you have your answer, start doing more of these things everyday and tell me how you feel afterwards.

Putting Yourself First

Some days you will forget about what makes you truly happy as you get bombarded by the harsh and cruel things life will throw at you. So I encourage you to put this list somewhere visible where you can see it everyday. Constantly remind yourself of what happiness means to you and shift your mind and body towards these actions every single day. I am sure you will be much happier person after that. See you in the next one :)

Chapter 7:

The Things That Matter

Today we're going to talk about a topic that I am very passionate about. Passionate because it has helped to guide each and every decision that I make on a daily basis. Having this constant reminder of the things that matter will put things in perspective for us - to eliminate the things that are taking up our time for the wrong reasons and to focus on the things that we actually want deep down in our hearts.

With that in mind, let's begin.

How many of you can safely say that you know what truly matters in life? How do you define living a successful and fulfilling life? Is it by having a certain net worth? Is it by living a stress-free life? Is it seeing the world? Is it by serving a defined number of people? Is it by having 10 life-long friends that you can count on? Is it by having a certain number of kids? Or have you not really thought about what you really want out of life yet?
Before we can really gear our actions towards the direction that we want to lead it, we must first know exactly what those specific things we want to achieve are.

The things that matter in my life vary over time as I get older and wiser. When I was young I used to think getting good grades, getting into a good university, and getting a good and stable job was all that really mattered, but I have soon come to realize that family, friends, and having people to hang out with were way more important than simply making money. There was a point in my life that I was so driven by money that I created a huge imbalance in my life by spending 99% of my time on my career. This lopsided drive caused me to neglect friendships, relationships, and soon people associated me with always being too busy for anything. I gradually stopped hanging out with anyone altogether. At first it was okay as I thought "hey, I finally have time to do whatever I want" and I don't have to be disturbed by meetups that would disrupt my workflow. But over time, I felt a gaping hole opening up somewhere deep inside that I could not seem to fill. I suddenly realized that I had successfully isolated myself from any and all relationships. This isolation felt increasingly lonely for me. I felt that I had no one to talk to when I was feeling down, no one to share my struggles with, no one to walk this journey with, and I knew I needed to do something about it. It was only after I started reconnecting with my friends did I truly feel alive again. Having friends brought me more joy than money ever did or could. There's a saying that you can't buy happiness; the same is true for friendships - you can't buy them either. They have to be earned and built with trust and loyalty.

For those of you who are so career focused and money-minded, I share from experience that the destination may not be pretty if you do not have friends or family to share it with. Sure you may afford a penthouse or a Ferrari, but what does it really mean? Sure you have a nice view and a fast ride, but can you share your life with it? When you are old and frail, can your house and car support you physically and emotionally? Don't make the same mistake I did for a good 3 years of my life. It was enough time for me to feel completely alone. No amount of acquiring things could fill that hole no matter how hard I tried. Sure I had the fanciest Apple products, my iPad, iPhone, MacBook, iMac, AirPods, the list goes on. Sure I could "make friends" with these shiny objects by using them everyday. But over time it just reminded me more and more that I had replaced people with gadgets, that I had replaced humans with Siri. It was really really sad honestly.

Having friends that don't judge you or who don't care whether you have money or not, those are the real friends that you know you can count on. And I urge those of you who have neglected this big part to start reconnecting old friends or finding new ones altogether who share the same interests as you. Golf buddies, tennis buddies, karaoke buddies, these are good places to start searching for friends and getting the ice broken.

If starting a family is something that you really want in life, have you begun searching for a partner and planning how and when you expect that to happen for you? Sure many of us think we may have a lot of time to do after we get our career going, but how many of us have heard stories of people who just never got off the bandwagon because they've become too busy with their careers? That maybe getting pregnant just never seems like the right time because you don't want to jeopardize your job. Or maybe that you never even got around to dating at all by the time you are 35 because you've become too busy being a general manager of your company. If having a career is the most important thing to you, then by all means go full steam ahead to achieve that goal. However if family is something of great significance to you, you may want to consider starting that timeline right now instead of waiting. Remember the goal is to focus on the things that truly matter. If having a loving spouse who you can grow old with and having say 2 kids who can support you when you are old is what you really want, maybe waiting isn't such a good idea. Finding love takes practice. You will meet frogs along the way and it takes time to grow a lasting relationship. Sure you can rush a marriage if time is of the essence, but is that ideal? Personally I believe a strong relationship takes 2-3 years to build. Do you have that type of runway to play with? Don't work yourself to death at your job only to find yourself rich and alone. Regret will come after for sure.

Whatever else you have defined as the things that matter to you, make sure that you never neglect those priorities. Sometimes life gets so busy and hectic that we forget to stop and refresh ourselves on what we really want to get out of life. It is all too easy for us to operate on autopilot - To set an alarm, go to work, gym, go home, take dinner, sleep, and repeat the day all over again. For weekends, we may be so exhausted from work that we just end up sleeping or wasting our weekend away only to begin the same routine again on Monday.

There's plenty of time for work decades down the road, but dating relationships and friendships may not have that runway of time.

So I challenge each and everyone of you to clearly define what the things that matter mean to you and to take consistent action in these areas day in and out until you can safely say you've already checked them off your bucket list. Take care and I'll see you in the next one.

Chapter 8:
Make Friends With Your Problems

Today we're going to talk about a topic that I hope will inspire you to view your problems not as a hurdle to your goals, but a necessity. How you can make friends with your problems to eventually see it as a part of your journey towards greater success.

You see, problems arise in all aspects of our lives every single day. As we go through life, we start to realise that life is merely about problem solving. When we are growing up, we face the problems of not being able to stand on our own two feet, problems about not being able to potty train, problems with peeing in the bed, problems with riding a new bicycle, problems with school, problems with Teachers, problems with our homework.

But the thing is that as kids, we view these problems as challenges. As something to work towards. We don't necessarily view problems as a negative thing, and we always strive to overcome these problems, never giving up until we do so. And through this perseverance, we grow and evolve. But as we get older, and our child-like response to problems start to change, we start seeing problems in a different way. Problems become obstacles rather than challenges, and problems sometimes overwhelm us to the point where we are not able to function.

We face problems in getting into good high schools and universities, problems in getting a job, problems with family, problems with relationships, problems with bosses, problems with colleagues, problems with starting a family. All these are legitimate problems that I am very sure every single one of us will face at some point in our lives. And the problems will never stop coming.

Putting Yourself First

From what I have shared so far, it is very clear that problems are a way of life, and problems will never go away. A life without problems is really not life at all.

Personally, I have dealt with my fair share of problems. I struggled greatly with getting good grades in university, I struggled in serving for the army as part of mandatory conscription for my country, I struggled with pressures from work, and these problems at times got to me where I felt that I could not see the light at the end of the tunnel. These problems consumed my vision that I could not see the big picture. That life is beautiful, and that my problems are nothing compared to what life has to offer.

In that moment as I was living through those problems however, I could not see the light. I was laser focused on the problem at hand and at many stages, I did feel depressed. I felt unworthy. I felt like I couldn't handle my problems.

I am not sure if my inability to handle problems as I grew older were genetic, or that my character just wasn't strong enough to withstand pressures from the external world. But I did feel like it became harder and harder each year.

What I failed to realise, and that goes back to how I saw problems when I was young, was that I viewed my problems as an enemy rather than a friend. I saw my problems as something that was getting in the way of my goals, rather than a necessary part of the process towards that goal.

By the time I was 20, I wanted a life without problems. I didn't want to deal with any more problems anymore. And as unrealistic as that sounded, I actually believed that it was what I wanted. And every problem that came my way felt like a mountain. A major annoyance that would take every ounce of my energy to overcome. And that negative view to problems actually made my life much more miserable.

It was only in my late twenties that I saw more of life did my perception of problems start to shift profoundly. I learned of the struggles that my parents had to go through to get the life that I was living today, I saw in many of my peers that work life is actually tough and those that viewed their job negatively almost always ended up depressed and unworthy while those that saw their work as challenges actually grew as people.

That shift happened gradually but I started to see the problems that came up in my daily life as friends rather than as enemies. I started to view the mandatory things I had to do to sustain myself financially, emotionally, physically, as simply a way of life. In areas such as health and fitness where I tend to struggle with a lot, which was quite a big problem in my opinion, i simply found alternative ways to keep fit that worked for me rather than get obsessed with the way i looked.

In areas of finance and career, where I also saw as a big problem, I adapted by adopting a completely novel way of working that actually made my work much more meaningful and enjoyable instead of subscribing myself to a job that I know that I would hate.

I started to view each problem as challenges again that would require my knowledge and expertise to overcome. And it started to consume me less and less. I made them my friends instead of my enemy. And when one door closes, I was always resourceful to find another open door to get me to where I wanted to go.

So I challenge each and everyone of you to start seeing your problems not as hindrances to your goals, but as challenges that requires your smartness to conquer. I believe that you have the power to knock down every problem that comes your way no matter how great the challenge is. However if it does become overwhelming, it is okay to walk away from it. Don't let it consume you and don't obsess over a problem until it wrecks your health mentally and physically. Life is too short for problems to ruin us. If it can't be made friends with, it is okay to simply let it go. Nothing good can come from sheer force.

I hope you have learned something today, and as always take care and I'll see you in the next one.

Chapter 9:
How To Take Action

Today we're going to talk about something pretty crucial. And this also plays into the topics of motivation, purpose, and goals. And that is, "How To Take Action". Before we begin, i want you to write down a couple of things that you were supposed to take action on but have been putting it off for whatever reason. And i want you to keep these things in mind as we go through this video. And hopefully by the end of it, i would have been able to convince you to take action and to start moving forward in your bigger life projects as well.

Why is Taking Action so important? To put it simply, taking action is the one thing that we can control to move us towards our goals. Whether we succeed or not is irrelevant in this case. Many of us hesitate to take action because we are afraid of failure. We fear the unknown and we over analyse and over think things to a point that we become paralysed. And I'm sure you guys have heard this term before: and that is analysis paralysis.

We draw up such detailed plans for how to are going to tackle this problem, we tweak and tweak the draft, aiming to find perfection before we even take the first action step to begin doing the work. And many times, for many people, we just let the plan sit on the shelves or in our computer, afraid to take action because we fear that we might not be able to accomplish the goal we have set out for ourselves.

You see, planning and drafting isn't going to move the needle. When we have a project, planning only makes up a small part of the process. And completion of the project is always down to every member of the group taking action and completing their part of the task. Or in the case of a solo project, all of the action and effort put in comes from you.

Putting Yourself First

When we plan for anything, even for our future, it is something that keeps us in check, to have a reference for us to know that we are on the right track. But whether or not we follow those plans are entirely up to the actions that we actually take. Whether we do save that $100 every month, or not spend money on unnecessary things, or say that we are going to invest in constant education and growth, these are not set in stone if we do not take action.

Another thing that holds us back from taking action is the fear that we will make mistakes. And that we will feel like a fool if we did things wrongly. But if you look at your life, realistically, how many times have you actually done something right the first time around on something that you haven't actually tried before? For example riding a bike, swimming, learning a new language, learning a new instrument. Wouldn't you agree that making mistakes is actually part of the process? Without practice there's not perfect, so why do we think that we will always get it right the first time when it comes to starting a new business or taking action on whatever new thing that we had set our sights on?

We have no problem telling ourselves that making mistakes in smaller things is okay but we berate ourselves or we create this immense expectation that we must get things right the first time around on bigger projects that we fear the climb because we fear the thought of falling down. And we don't even give ourselves a chance to prove that we can do it.

To counter this, we must tell ourselves that making mistakes is a part of the process, to not rush the process, and to give ourselves more room for failure so that we will have the best chance of actually succeeding someday. However long it takes. We must trust the process because it will happen for us eventually. The only time we really do fail is the last time we actually stop trying, stop taking action, and stop learning from our mistakes. that is the time when we can say we are a failure, if we quit. But if we never give up, and we keep taking action, it will work out for us.

Putting Yourself First

One final hurdle that many of us face is that we tend to want to rush the process and we set unrealistic deadlines to achieve those goals. If we go back to our previous example of learning a new instrument, how many of you guys will agree that, although not impossible, it is unrealistic to become a guitar guru after the 1st year? Most of us would realistically say that it will take at least a few years of daily practice to actually become a pro guitar player. But how many of us actually apply that same concept to a big project like growing our income from $3k to $10k. We all expect fast results and fast growth, but rarely does things work out so smoothly, unless we are incredibly lucky.

When we set these big targets but fail to realise that we need to take baby steps consistently everyday, we set ourselves up for failure without realising it. Without giving ourselves the room to grow a seed into a tree, we end up chopping it down when it is still at the early growth stages. And we fail to let time and effort do it's thing, giving it water and light day in and day out. And we beat ourselves up when we quit prematurely.

What I have learnt, from experience, is that the best way to achieve something eventually, is to take baby steps, taking a little action each day, be it 5 mins, an hour, or 10 hours, they all count. And instead of just hoping to rush to the end, that I actually learned to not only enjoy the process, but also to trust that my efforts will all pay off in the end. And many a times, they did. I left the fear and worry to one side and just focused on taking action. I stopped comparing myself with my peers, and focused on my own journey. I can't control how much faster my competition can grow or achieve, but i can definitely control my own destiny.

So i challenge each and everyone of you today to take a look at the list of things that you hope to achieve that you have written down at the start of this video, and to take the first step of stop trying to perfect the plan, to stop thinking and worrying about what might and could go wrong, to stop fearing the unknown, and to simply just take a little action each day. The worse thing that you can do to yourself is to not even try. You will make mistakes along the way, but as long as you learn from them, you will be moving in the right direction.

Chapter 10:
Happy People Do What Matters to Them

Think about what you want most out of life. What were you created for? What is your mission in life? What is your passion? You were put on this earth for a reason, and knowing that reason will help you determine your priorities.

I spent a total of four months in the hospital, healing from my sickness. During that time, I spent a lot of time thinking about my purpose in life. I discovered that my purpose is to help you change your lives by focusing on what matters most to you.

1. **Create A Plan**

Create a plan to get from where you are today to where you want to be. Maybe you need a new job. Maybe you need to go back to school. Maybe you need to deal with some relationship issues. Whatever it is, create a plan that will get you to where you want to be.

While I was in the hospital, I began to draft my life plan. My plan guides all of my actions, helps me focus on my relationships with my wife and daughter, and helps me keep working toward my life purpose. A life plan will help you focus your life too.

2. **Focus On Now**

Stop multitasking and focus on one thing at a time. It may be a project at work. It may be a conversation with your best friend. It may just be the book that you have wanted to read for months. The key is to focus on one thing at a time.

I plan each day the night before by picking the three most important tasks from my to-do list. In the morning, I focus on each one of these tasks individually until they are completed. Once I complete these three tasks, I check email, return phone calls, etc.

3. Just Say "No."

We all have too much to do and too little time. The only way you will find the time for the things that matter is to say "no" to the things that don't.

I use my purpose and life plan to make decisions about the projects and tasks I say yes to. If a project or task is not aligned with my purpose, a good fit with my life plan, and sometimes that I have time to accomplish, I say no to the project. Saying no to good opportunities gives you time to focus on the best opportunities.

Research tells us that 97 percent of people are living their life by default and not by design. They don't know where their life is headed and don't plan what they want to accomplish in life.

These steps will help you to decide what matters most to you. They will help you to begin living your life by design and not by default. Most importantly, they will help you to create a life focused on what matters to you.

Let me end by asking, "What matters most to you?

Putting Yourself First

PART 3

Chapter 1:
Being 100% Happy Is Overrated

Lately I've been feeling as though happiness isn't something that truly lasts. Happiness isn't something that will stay with us very long. We may feel happy when we are hanging out with friends, but that feeling will eventually end once we part for the day. I've been feeling as though expecting to be constantly happy is very overrated. We try to chase this idea of being happy. We chase the material possessions, we chase the fancy cars, house, and whatever other stuff that we think will make us happy. But more often than not the desire is never really fulfilled. Instead, i believe that the feeling accomplishment is a much better state of mind to work towards. Things will never make us happy. We may enjoy the product we have worked so hard for temporarily. But that feeling soon goes away. And we are left wondering what is the next best thing we can aim our sights on. This never-ending chase becomes a repetitive cycle, one that we never truly are aware of but constantly desire. We fall into the trap that finding happiness is the end all-be-all.

What i've come to realise is that most of the time, we are actually operating on a more baseline level. A state that is skewed more towards the neutral end. Neither truly happy, or neither truly sad. And I believe that is perfectly okay. We should allow ourselves to embrace and accept the fact that it is okay to be just fine. Just neutral. Sure it isn't something very exciting, but we shouldn't put ourselves in a place where we expect to be constantly happy in order to lead a successful life. This revelation came when I realised that every time I felt happy, I would experience a crash in mood the next day. I would start looking at instagram, checking up on my friends, comparing their days, and thinking that they are leading a happier life than I was. I would then start berating myself and find ways to re-create those happy moments just for the sake of it. Just because I thought i needed to feel happy all the time. It was only when I actually sat down and started looking inwards did I realise that maybe I can never truly find happiness from external sources.

Instead of trying to find happiness in things and external factors that are beyond my control, I started looking for happiness from within myself. I began to appreciate how happy I was simply being alone. Being by myself. Not letting other factors pull me down. I found that I was actually happiest when I was taking a long shower, listening to my own thoughts. No music playing, no talking to people, just me typing away on my computer, writing down all the feelings I am feeling, all the thoughts that I am thinking, letting every emotion I was feeling out of my system. I started to realise that the lack of distractions, noise, comparisons with others, free from social media, actually provided me with a clearer mind. It was in those brief moments where I found myself to be my most productive, with ideas streaming all over the place. It was in that state of mind that I did feel somewhat happy. That I could create that state of mind without depending on other people to fulfil it for me.

If any of you out there feel that your emotions are all over the place, maybe it is time for you to sit down by yourself for a little while. Stop searching for happiness in things and stuff, and sometimes even people. We think it is another person's job to make us happy. We expect to receive compliments, flowers, a kiss, in order to feel happy. While those things are certainly nice to have, being able to find happiness from within is much better. By sitting and reflecting in a quiet space, free from any noise and distractions, we may soon realise that maybe we are okay being just okay. Maybe we don't need expensive jewellery or handbags or fancy houses to make us happy. Maybe we just need a quiet mind and a grateful spirit.

The goal is to find inner peace. To accept life for the way it is. To accept things as the way they are. To be grateful for the things we have. That is what it means to be happy.

Chapter 2:
The Trick To Focusing

If you've been struggling with procrastinations and distractions, just not being able to do the things you know you should do and purposefully putting them off by mindlessly browsing social media or the web, then today I'm going to share with you one very simple trick that has worked for me in getting myself to focus.

I will not beat around the bush for this. The trick is to sit in silence for a minute with your work laid out in front of you in a quiet place free from noise or distractions. I know it sounds silly, but it has worked time and time again for me whenever I did this and I believe it will work the same for you.

You see our brains are constantly racing with a million thoughts. Thoughts telling us whether we should be doing our work, thoughts telling us that we should turn on the TV instead, thoughts that don't serve any real purpose but to pull us away from our goal of doing the things that matter.

Instead of being a victim of our minds, and going according to its whims and fancies. Quieting down the mind by sitting in complete silence is a good way to engage ourselves in a deeper way. A way that cuts the mind off completely, to plug ourselves out of the automated thoughts that don't serve us, and to realign ourselves with our goals and purpose of working.

To do this effectively, it is best that you turn on the AC to a comfortable temperature, sit on your working chair, lay your work out neatly in front of you, and just sit in silence for a moment. What I found that works a step up is to actually put on my noise cancelling headphones, and I find myself disappear into a clear mind. A mind free from noise, distractions, social media, music, and all the possible ways that it can throw me off my focus.

With no noise whatsoever, you will find yourself at complete peace with the world. Your thoughts about procrastination will get crushed by your feelings of serenity and peace. A feeling that you can do anything if you wanted to right now.

Everytime I turned on music or the TV, thinking I needed it as a distraction, my focus always ends up split. I operate on a much lower level of productivity because my mind is in two places. One listening to the TV or music, and the other on my work. I end up wasting more resources of my brain and end up feeling more tired and fatigued quickly than I normally would.

If that sounds familiar to you, well i have been there and done that too. And I can tell you that it is not a sustainable way to go about doing things in the long run.

The power of silence is immense. It keeps us laser focused on the task in front of us. And we hesitate less on every decision.

The next thing I would need you to do is to actually challenge yourself to be distraction free for as long as possible when you first start engaging in silence. Put all your devices on silent mode, keep it vibration free, and do not let notifications suck you back into the world of distractions. It is the number 1 killer of productivity and focus for all of us.

So if u struggle with focusing, I want you to give it a try right. If you know you are distracted there is no harm right here right now to make a choice to give this a shot.

Take out our noise cancelling earphones, turn the ac on, turn your devices off or to silent, lay your work out in front of you, turn up the lights, sit on your chair, close your eyes for a minute, and watch the magic happen.

Chapter 3:
Having a Balanced Life

Today we're going to talk about how and why you should strive to achieve a balanced life. A balance between work, play, family, friends, and just time alone to yourself.

We all tend to lead busy lives. At some points we shift our entire focus onto something at the expense of other areas that are equally important.

I remember the time when I just got a new office space. I was so excited to work that i spent almost 95% of the week at the office. I couldn't for the life of me figured why i was so addicted to going to the office that I failed to see I was neglecting my family, my friends, my relationships. Soon after the novelty effect wore off, i found myself burnt out, distant from my friends and family, and sadly also found myself in a strained relationship.

This distance was created by me and me alone. I had forgotten what my priorities were. I hadn't realized that I had thrown my life completely off balance. I found myself missing the time I spent with my family and friends. And I found myself having to repair a strained relationship due to my lack of care and concern for the other party.

What you think is right in the moment, to focus on something exclusively at the expense of all else, may seem enticing. It may seem like there is nothing wrong with it. But dig deeper and check to make sure it is truly worth the sacrifice you are willing to make in other areas of your life.

It is easy for us to fall into the trap of wanting to make more money, wanting to work harder, to be career driven and all that. But what is the point in having more money if

Putting Yourself First

you don't have anyone to spend in on or spend it with? What's the point in having a nice car or a nice designer handbag if you don't have anyone to show it to?

Creating balance in our lives is a choice. We have the choice to carve out time in our schedule for the things that truly matter. Only when we know how to prioritise our day, our week, our month, can we truly find consistency and stability in our lives.

I know some people might say disagree with what I am sharing with you all today, but this is coming from my personal life experience. It was only after realising that I had broken down all the things I had worked so hard to build prior to this new work venture, that I started to see the bigger picture again.

That I didn't want to go down this path and find myself 30 years later regretting that I had not spent time with my family before they passed away, that I was all alone in this world without someone I can lean my shoulder on to walk this journey with me, that I didn't have any friends that I could call up on a Tuesday afternoon to have lunch with me because everyone thought of me as a flaker who didn't prioritise them in the their lives before.

Choose the kind of life you want for yourself. If what I have to say resonates with you, start writing down the things that you know you have not been paying much attention to lately because of something else that you chose to do. Whether it be your lover, your friends, a hobby, a passion project, whatever it may be. Start doing it again. The time to create balance is now.

Chapter 4:
Enjoying The Journey

Today I want to talk about why enjoying the journey of life is important. And why hurrying to get to the destination might not be all that enjoyable as we think it is.

A lot of us plan our lives around an end goal, whether it be getting to a particular position in our company's ladder, or becoming the best player in a sport, or having the most followers on Instagram or whatever the goal may be... Many of us just can't wait to get there. However, many a times, once we reach our goal, whilst we may feel a sense of satisfaction and accomplishment for a brief moment, we inevitably feel like something is missing again and we search for our next objective and target to hit.

I have come to realise that in life, it is not always so much the end goal, but the journey, trials, struggles, and tribulations that make the journey there worth it. If we only focus on the end goal, we may miss out the amazing sights along the way. We will ultimately miss the point of the journey and why we embarked on it in the first place.

Athletes who achieve one major title never stop at just that one, they look for the next milestone they can achieve, but they enjoy the process, they take it one step at a time and at the end of their careers they can look back with joy that they had left no stone unturned. And that they can live their life without regret.

How many times have you seen celebrities winning the biggest prize in their careers, whether it may be the Grammy's Album of the Year if you are a musician, or the Oscars Best Actor or Best Actress Award. How many of them actually feel like that is the end of the journey? They keep creating and keep making movies and film not because they

Putting Yourself First

want that award, even though it is certainly a nice distinction to have, but more so because they enjoy their craft and they enjoy the art of producing.

If winning that trophy was the end goal, we would see many artists just end their careers there and then after reaching the summit. However that is not the case. They will try to create something new for as long as people are engaged with their craft, as with the case of Meryl Streep, even at 70+ she is still working her butt off even after she has achieve all the fame and money in the world.

Even for myself, at times i just want to reach the end as quickly as possible. But many times when i get there, i am never satisfied. I feel empty inside and i feel that I should be doing more. And when i rush to the end, i do feel like I missed many important sights along the way that would have made the journey much more rewarding and enjoyable had I told myself to slow it down just a little.

I believe that for all of us, the journey is much more important than the destination. It is through the journey that we grow as a person, it is through the journey that we evolve and take on new ideas, work ethics, knowledge, and many little nuggets that make the trip worth it at the end. If someone were to hand you a grand slam title without having you earned it, it would be an empty trophy with no meaning and emotions behind it. The trophy would not represent the hours of hard work that you have put in to be deserving of that title.

So I challenge each and everyone of you today to take a step back in whatever journey you may be on. To analyse in what aspects can you enjoy the moment and to not place so much pressure into getting to the destination asap. Take it one day at a time and see how the journey you are on is actually a meaningful one that you should treasure each day and not let up.

I hope you enjoyed today's topic and sharing and as always I wish you all the best in your endeavours. I'll see you in the next one.

Chapter 5:
Don't Make Life Harder Than It Needs To Be

Today we're going to talk about a topic that I hope will inspire you to make better decisions and to take things more lightly. As we go through this journey of life together, and as we get older, we soon find ourselves with more challenges that we need to face, more problems that we need to solve, and more responsibilities that we need to take on as an adult. In each phase of life, the bar gets set higher for us. When we are young, our troubles mostly revolve around school and education. For most of us we don't have to worry much about making money or trying to provide for a family, although I know that some of you who come from lesser well off families might have had to start doing a lot earlier. And to you i commend you greatly. For the rest of us we deal with problems with early teenage dating, body image, puberty, grades, and so on. It is only until we graduate from university do we face the harsh reality of the real world. Of being a working adult. It is only then are we really forced to grow up. To face nasty colleagues, bosses, customers, you name it. And that is only just the beginning.

Life starts to get more complicated for many of us when we start to realise that we have to manage our own finances now. When our parents stop giving us money and that we only have ourselves to rely on to survive. Suddenly reality hits us like a truck. We realise that making our own money becomes our primary focus and that we may not have much else to rely on. We take on loans, mortgages, credit card debts, and it seems to never really end. For many of us, we may end up in a rat race that we can't get out of because of the payments and loans that we have already ended up committing to. The things we buy have a direct impact on the obligations that have to maintain.

Putting Yourself First

Next we have to worry about finding a partner, marriage, starting a family, buying a house, providing for your kids, setting aside money for their growth, college fund, the list goes on and on.

Do you feel overwhelmed with this summary of the first maybe one-third of your life? The reality is that that is probably the exact time line that most of us will eventually go through. The next phase of life requires us to keep up the payments, to go to our jobs, to keep making that dough to sustain our family. We may have to also make enough money to pay for tuition fees, holidays, gifts, payments to parents, and whatever other commitments that we might have. And this might go on until we reach 60, when two-thirds of our lives are already behind us.

Life as you can see, without any external help, is already complicated enough. If you didn't already know by now, life isn't easy. Life is full of challenges, obligations, obstacles, commitments, and this is without any unforeseen events that might happen... Medical or family wise.

With all this in mind, why do we want to make life harder than it already is?

Every additional decision that you make on top of this list will only add to your burden, if it is not the right one, and every person that you add into your life that is negative will only bring the experience much less enjoyable.

To make life easier for you and your soul, I recommend that you choose each step wisely. Choose carefully the partner that you intend to spend your life with, choose wisely the people that you choose to spend your time with, choose wisely the food that you put in your body, and choose wisely the life that you wish to lead.

Be absolutely clear on the vision that you have for your life because it ain't easy.

Another thing to make your life much less complicated is to put less pressure on yourself. I believe that you don't need to start comparing your life with others because

Putting Yourself First

everyone is on their own journey. Don't chase the fancy houses and cars that your friends have just because they have them. Everyone is different and everyone's priorities might be different as well. They might pride having a luxury car over spending on other areas of life, which might differ from the interests that you might have. Comparison will only most certainly lead you to chase a life that you might not even want to attain. And you might lose your sleep and mind trying to match up to your peers. Focus on yourself instead and on exactly what you want out of life and it will definitely be enough.

I challenge each and everyone of you to have a clear set of priorities for yourself. And once you have done so and are working towards those goals, be contented about it. Don't change the goalpost just because your friends say you must, or because you are jealous of what they have. Be satisfied in your own path and life will reward you with happiness as well.

I hope you learned something today. Thank you and I'll see you in the next one.

Chapter 6:
Practicing Visualisation For Your Goals

Today we're going to talk about visualisation and why I think all of you should practice some form of visualisation everyday to help keep you on track to the future that you can see yourself living in maybe 5 or 10 years down the road.

So before we begin today's video, i want you to write down some of the goals that you want to achieve. These goals need not be entirely monetary, it could also be finding a partner, having a kid, having lots of friends, playing in a tournament of some elite sport, playing fluent guitar, skateboarding like a pro, or even working at the Apple store maybe... any personal goals and dreams that you might think u want.

And In terms of monetary goals, it could be the kind of income level and the kinds of material possessions that you wish you had, for example a dream car of yours, a pretty landed house or apartment in a prestigious neighbourhood, and nice flat screen Tv, a 10k diamond ring. Or whatever it may be. No matter how ridiculous, i want you to write these down.

Alright now that we have got this list in your hands, lets talk about what visualisation is and how it can be a powerful tool to help you actually achieve your goals.

What visualisation essentially is in a nutshell, is that it helps you step into the shoes of your future self, whether that may be 10 mins in the future, 10 years into the future, or even when you are at your death bed.

Putting Yourself First

So why would we want to even think or imagine ourselves in the future when people have been telling us to be present and living in the moment etc. People including myself in my other videos. Well you see, the difference is that with visualisation, we are not looking into our past successes and failures as factors that influence our present state of mind, but rather to create a picture of a person that we want to be in the future that we can be proud of. A person that we think and aspire to become. Whether that be emulating an already rich or successful person, or simply just choosing to see yourself in possession of these things and people that you want in your life. Visualisation can help us mentally prepare ourselves for our future and help us solidify and affirm the actions that we need to take right now at this very moment to get to that end point.

Visualisation is such a powerful tool that when done correctly and consistency, our brain starts to blur the line between our present reality and our future self. And we are able to retrain and rewire our brain to function in the way that helps us achieve those goals by taking action more readily. If we have chosen to visualise ourselves as a pro tennis player, however far fetched it may seem, we have already decided on some level deep down that we are going to become that person no matter what it takes. And on a mental level, we have already committed to practicing the sport daily to achieve that outcome. If it is an income goal we hope to achieve, by visualising the person we hope to become who earns maybe $100k a month, yes it might sound far fetched again, but it is certainly not impossible, we will take actions that are drastically different than what we are doing today to make that goal happen. A person who visualises themselves making $100k a month will say and do things that are completely different from someone who tells themselves that they are okay to make just $2000 a month.

The action and effort taken is on a whole other level. A person who says they want to stay an amateur tennis player will do things differently than someone who visualises themselves becoming the top player of the sport who is ready to win grand slams.

With these two examples in mind, now i want you to take that list that we have created at the start of the video, and i want you to now place yourself inside of your imagination, I want you to start picturing a future you that has already been there done that. A future

Putting Yourself First

you who has got everything that he ever wanted, friends, family, money, career, sports, hobbies, travel, seeing the world, all of it. And I want you to visualise how you actually got to that point. What were the actions that you took to get there. How much time did you have to spend on each activity each day, day in and day out, and the level of commitment and desire that you needed to have, the belief that you will and have achieved your wildest dreams, how that must have felt, the emotion associated with reaching your goals, and becoming the person that you've always known you could be.

As this is your first time, i want you to spend at least 5-10mins trying to see yourself in your future shoes. It might not come right away as even visualisation takes practice. When we are so used to not using our imagination, it can be hard to reactivate that part of the brain. If you do not see it right now, i want you to keep going at it daily until that person in your head becomes clearer and clearer to you.

It might be easier to just see yourself as the next Warren Buffet, Jeff Bezos, Steve Jobs, Roger Federer, or whoever idol and superstar you wish to emulate. When you aim to emulate their success, you will mimic the actions that they take, and that could be a good way to start. Even a small change in your attitude and actions can go a long way.

Now that you have had a taste of the power of visualisation, I want you to practice visualisation on a daily basis. Again, everything boils down to consistency, and the more u practice seeing yourself as a successful person in life regularly, the more you believe that you can get there. Try your very best to pair that feeling with immense emotion. The feeling you get when you finally reached the summit. It will give you the best chance of success at actually following through with your goals and dreams.

To keep yourself motivated each day to practice visualisation, click on this link and save it to your favourites of daily habits. Refer to meditation series.

This has been quite an interesting topic to make for me as I have used visualisation myself with great success in helping me take consistent action, something that I struggle with daily, to reprogram my mind to work hard and stay the path.

Chapter 7:
Happy People Live Slow

"Slow Living means **structuring your life around meaning and fulfilment**. Similar to 'voluntary simplicity and 'downshifting,' it emphasizes a **less-is-more approach**, focusing on the quality of your life...Slow Living addresses the desire to lead a more balanced life and pursue a **more holistic sense of well-being** in the fullest sense of the word. In addition to the personal advantages, there are potential **environmental benefits** as well. When we slow down, we often use fewer resources and produce less waste, both of which have a lighter impact on the earth."

Slow living is a state of mind it will make you feel purposeful and is more fulfilling. It is all about being consistent and steady. Now that you have an idea of slow living, we will break down some myths attached to slow living and how to start slow living for mind peace and happiness. The first myth is that slow living is about doing everything as slowly as possible. Slow living is not about doing everything in slow motion but doing things at the right speed and not rushing. It is all about gaining time so you can do things that are important to you. The second myth is that slow living is the same as simple living. Now simple living is more worldly, and simple living is more focused on time.

The third myth is that slow living is an aesthetic that you see on desaturated Instagram posts, but that is not true; this is considered a minimalist aesthetic, whereas slow living is a minimalist lifestyle. The 4th myth is that slow living is about doing and being less. That is not at all true. It is all about removing the non-essentials from your life so you can have more time to be yourself. And the last myth is that slow living is anti-technology now. This is not about travelling back in time but all about using tech as a tool and not vice versa.

If you like this idea of living, we are going to list ten ways in which you can start slow living;

1. Define what is most important to you(essentials)
2. Say no to everything else (non-essentials)
3. Understand busyness and that it is a choice
4. Create space and margin in your day and life
5. Practice being present
6. Commit to putting your life before work
7. Adopt a slow information diet
8. Get outside physically and connect dots mentally
9. Start slow and small by downshifting
10. Find inspiration in the slow living community

Sit back and think about what the purpose of your life is, what you ultimately want from your life and not just in a monetary sense. Think about what you would like for your lifestyle to be 50 years from now, and then start working on it today. Suppose you have not figured out the purpose. In that case, there are multiple personality tests available on the internet that will help you determine your personality type and then eventually help you create your purpose.

Chapter 8:
7 Ways To Know If You're A Good Person

This question is something that we wonder from time to time. When we are at our lowest point and we look around, there could be a chance that there may not be that many people in our lives that we can really count on.

We start to wonder how people actually see us. Are we good people? Have we been nice to those around us? Or do we come off as pretentious and hence people tend to stay clear of us for some reason.

There is a dilemma lately about the use of social media and having followers. It seems that people are interested in following your socials, but when it comes to you asking them out or chatting them up, they don't respond or are uninterested to meet up with you.

You then start to wonder if there is something wrong with you. You start to question your morals, your self-worth, and everything about your life. This can quickly spiral out of control and lead to feelings that you are somehow flawed.

Today we're going to help you answer that question: Am I a good person? Here are 7 Ways To Find Out If You Are Indeed One

1. Look At The People Who Have Stuck Around

I think this one is a good place to start for all of us. Instead of wondering if we have gone wrong somewhere, take a look at the friends and family who have stuck around for you over all this time. They are still there for you for a reason. You must have done something right for them not to leave you for other people. Sure some of them may not be as close as they once were, but they are still there. Think about the people who celebrate your birthdays with you, the people who still asks if you want to hang out from time to time, and the people who you can count on in times of emergency. We may not be able to determine if we are good people from this, but we know that at least we are not so far off the rails.

2. Ask Them To Be Honest With You

If you really want to find out if you are a good person, ask your friends directly and honestly, to point out to you areas that they feel you need to work on. Sometimes we cannot see the flaws and the misguided actions that we portray to the world. People may gradually dislike and drift away from us quietly without telling us why. The people who have stuck around know you best, so let them be brutally honest with you. Take what they have to say as constructive criticism, rather than a personal attack on your character. It is better to know in what areas you lack as a person and to work to improve it, than to go through life obliviously and thinking that there is absolutely nothing wrong with you.

3. Think About Why Your Friends May Not Respond To Your Messages

Many a times friendships simply run its natural course. As work, relationships, and family come into the picture, it is inevitable that people drift apart over time. If you decide to hit your friends up and they don't respond, don't take it too personally. It could be that maybe you're just not a vital piece of the puzzle in their lives anymore. If their friendships aren't one that you have been cultivating anyway, you may want to consider removing them completely from your lives. Find new people who will appreciate and love you rather than dwell on the past. There may be nothing wrong with you as a person, it's just the cruel nature of time playing its dirty game.

Putting Yourself First

4. Keeping It Real With Yourself

Do you think that you are a good person? The fact that you are here shows that you may already have an inclination that something may not be quite right with you but you can't quite put a finger on it. Instead of looking for confirmation from external sources, try looking within. Ask yourself the hard questions. Think about every aspect of your life and evaluate yourself. If you have more enemies than friends, maybe there is something you aren't doing quite right that needs some work. Write those possible flaws down and see if you can work through them.

5. Do You Try Your Best To Help Others?

Sometimes we may not be great friends but we may be great at other things, such as being passionate about a cause or helping other people. Maybe friendships aren't a priority for us and hence it is not a good indicator of whether we are good people by looking at the quality of our friendships. If instead we are driven by a cause bigger than ourselves, and we participate through volunteering, events, and donation drives, we can pat ourselves on the back and say that at least we have done something meaningful to better the lives of others. In my opinion you are already a winner.

6. Is Life Always About What You Want?

This one could be a red flag because if we create a life that is only centred around us, we are in danger of being self-obsessive. Having the "Me First" attitude isn't something to be proud of. Life is about give and take, and decisions should be made fairly for all parties involved. If you only want to do things your way, or go to places you want, at the expense of the opinions of others, you are driving people away without realising it. Nobody likes someone who only thinks about themselves. If you catch yourself in this position, it may be time to consider a 180 turn.

7. People Enjoy Being Around You

Putting Yourself First

While this may not be the best indicator that you are a good person, it is still a decent way to tell if you are well-liked and if people enjoy your presence. Generally people are attracted to others who are kind, loyal, trustworthy, and charismatic. If people choose to ask you out, they could find you to be one of those things, which is a good sign that you're not all too bad. Of course you could have ulterior motives for presenting yourself in a well-liked manner, but disingenuity usually gets found out eventually and you very well know if you are being deceitful to others for your own personal gain.

Conclusion

There is no sure-fire way to tell if you are a good person. No one point can be definitive. But you can definitely look at a combination of factors to determine the possibility of that age-old question. The only thing you can do is to constantly work on improving yourself. Invest time and effort into becoming a better person and never stop striving for growth in your character.

Chapter 9:
Constraints Make You Better: Why the Right Limitations Boost Performance

It is not uncommon to complain about the constraints in your life. Some people say that they have little time, money, and resources, or their network is limited. Yes, some of these things can hold us back, but there is a positive side to all of this. These constraints are what forces us to make choices and cultivate talents that can otherwise go undeveloped. Constraints are what drives creativity and foster skill development. In many ways reaching the next level of performance is simply a matter of choosing the right constraints.

How to Choose the Right Constraints

There are three primary steps that you can follow when you are using constraints to improve your skills.

1. **Decide what specific skill you want to develop.**

The more specific you are in the skill, the easier it will be to design a good constraint for yourself. You shouldn't try to develop the skill of being "good at marketing," for example. It's too broad. Instead, focus on learning how to write compelling headlines or analyze website data—something specific and tangible.

2. **Design a constraint that requires this specific skill to be used**

There are three main options for designing a constraint: time, resources, and environment.

- **Time:** Give yourself less time to accomplish a task or set a schedule that forces you to work on skills more consistently.

- **Resources:** Give yourself fewer resources (or different resources) to do a task.

- **Environment:** According to one study, if you eat on 10-inch plates rather than 12-inch plates, you'll consume 22 percent fewer calories over a year. One simple change in the environment can lead to significant results. In my opinion, environmental constraints are best because they impact your behavior without you realizing it.

3. **Play the game**

Constraints can accelerate skill development, but they aren't a magic pill. You still need to put in your time. The best plan is useless without repeated action. What matters most is getting your reps in.

The idea is to practice, experiment with different constraints to boost your skills. As for myself, I am working on storytelling skills these days. I have some friends who are amazing storytellers. I've never been great at it, but I'd like to get better. The constraint I've placed on myself is scheduling talks without the use of slides. My last five speaking engagements have used no slides or a few basic images. Without text to rely on, I have designed a constraint that forces me to tell better stories so that I don't embarrass myself in front of the audience.

So, the question here is What do you want to become great at? What skills do you want to develop? Most importantly, what constraints can you place upon yourself to get there? Figure these things out and start from today!

Why You Are Amazing

When was the last time you told yourself that you were amazing? Was it last week, last month, last year, or maybe not even once in your life?

As humans, we always seek to gain validation from our peers. We wait to see if something that we did recently warranted praise or commendation. Either from our colleagues, our bosses, our friends, or even our families. And when we don't receive those words that we expect them to, we think that we are unworthy, or that our work just wasn't good enough. That we are lousy and under serving of praise.

With social media and the power of the internet, these feelings have been amplified. For those of us that look at the likes on our Instagram posts or stories, or the number of followers on Tiktok, Facebook, or Snapchat, we allow ourselves to be subjected to the validation of external forces in order to qualify our self-worth. Whether these are strangers who don't know you at all, or whoever they might be, their approval seems to matter the most to us rather than the approval we can choose to give ourselves.

Putting Yourself First

We believe that we always have to up our game in order to seek happiness. Everytime we don't get the likes, we let it affect our mood for the rest of the day or even the week.

Have you ever thought of how wonderful it is if you are your best cheerleader in life? If the only validation you needed to seek was from yourself? That you were proud of the work you put out there, even if the world disagrees, because you know that you have put your heart and soul into the project and that there was nothing else you could have done better in that moment when you were producing that thing?

I am here to tell you that you are amazing because only you have the power to choose to love yourself unconditionally. You have the power to tell yourself that you are amazing. and that you have the power to look into yourself and be proud of how far you came in life. To be amazed by the things that you have done up until this point, things that other people might not have seen, acknowledged, or given credit to you for. But you can give that credit to yourself. To pat yourself on the back and say "I did a great job".

I believe that we all have this ability to look inwards. That we don't need external forces to tell us we are amazing because deep down, we already know we are.

If nobody else in the world loves you, know that I do. I love your courage, your bravery, your resilience, your heart, your soul, your commitment, and your dedication to live out your best life on this earth. Tell yourself each and everyday that you deserve to be loved, and that you are loved.

Go through life fiercely knowing that you don't need to seek happiness, validations, and approval from others. That you have it inside you all along and that is all you need to keep going.

Chapter 10:
<u>Believe in Yourself</u>

Listen up. I want to tell you a story. This story is about a boy. A boy who became a man, despite all odds. You see, when he was a child, he didn't have a lot going for him. The smallest and weakest in his class, he had to struggle every day just to keep up with his peers. Every minute of every hour was a fight against an opponent bigger and stronger than he was - and every day he was knocked down. Beaten. Defeated. But... despite that... despite everything that was going against him... this small, weak boy had one thing that separated him from hundreds of millions of people in this world. A differentiating factor that made a difference in the matter of what makes a winner in this world of losers. You see this boy believed in himself. No matter the odds, he believed fundamentally that he had the power to overcome anything that got in his way! It didn't matter how many times he was knocked down, he got RIGHT BACK UP!

Now it wasn't easy. It hurt like hell. Every time he failed was another reminder of how far behind he was. A reminder of the nearly insurmountable gap between him and everyone else and lurking behind that reminder was the temptation, the suggestion to just give up. Throw in the towel. Surrender the win. Yet believe me when I tell you that no matter HOW tough things got, no matter HOW much he wanted to give in, a small voice in his heart keep saying... not today... just once more... I know it hurts but I can try again... Just. Once. More.

You see more than anything in this world HE KNEW that deep inside him was a greatness just WAITING to be tapped into! A power that most people would never see, but not him. It didn't matter what the world threw at him, because he'd be damned if he let his potential die alongside him. And all it took? All it required to unlock the chasm of greatness inside was a moment to realise the lies the world tried to tell him. In less than a second he recognised the light inside that would ignite a spark of success to address the ones who didn't believe that he could do it. The ones who told him to give up! Get out! Go home and roam the streets where failure meets those who weren't born to sit at the seat at the top!

Yet what they didn't know is that being born weak didn't matter any longer 'cause in his fight to succeed he became stronger. Rising up to the heights beyond, he WOULD NOT GIVE UP till he forged a bond within his heart that ensured NO MATTER THE ODDS, no matter what anyone said about him, no matter what the world told him, he had something that NO ONE could take away from him. A power so strong it transformed this boy into a man. A loser into a winner. A failure into a success. That, is the power of self-belief...

CPSIA information can be obtained
at www.ICGtesting.com
Printed in the USA
BVHW042043120122
626091BV00008B/30